Dorking
in old picture postcards

by
Greta Morley

European Library – Zaltbommel/Netherlands

GB ISBN 90 288 4738 3 / CIP

© 1989 European Library – Zaltbommel/Netherlands

No part of this book may be reproduced in any form, by print, photoprint, microfilm or any other means without written permission from the publisher.

INTRODUCTION

Dorking and its surrounding district has often been described as the 'Switzerland of England'. Certainly it can lay claim to some of the most picturesque scenery to be found anywhere in the south of England.

Happily, we have been spared the fate which has befallen other erstwhile beauty spots. While their glory is a thing of the past, the Dorking area still offers incomparable advantages as a peaceful haven. It has few equals with the pure and exhilarating air of the hills which encompass the town on either side.

Though Dorking town lies in a valley, it has an altitude of about 200 feet above sea level, while Box Hill is 600 feet, Ranmore 620 feet and Leith Hill 965 feet.

We first find mention of Dorking in the Domesday Book. It was then called 'Dorchings', and at a later period 'Darking'. The derivation of the word is not easy to determine, nor is it necessary to dwell on the suggestions which have been put forward. That it is a town rich in historical associations is, however, quite certain. For instance, it is clear that the Old Roman road, called Stane Street, passed through the town on its way to the coast. Historians have sufficiently located it, at least to their own satisfaction, as to aver that its course lay to the west of St. Martin's Parish churchyard. The famous Pilgrims Way, is also said to have passed through the outskirts of the town.

Dorking clings to its old traditions with a highly protective Preservation Society that grows from strength to strength. People born and bred in the town are still called 'five clawed 'uns' after a breed of fowls for which Dorking is noted.

The town has associations with many famous residents. John Keats finished his 'Endymion' at the inn at Burford Bridge; 'Parson Malthus', the population economist, lived at the Rookery in 1776; Sheridan once resided at Polesden and Daniel Defoe lived in the neighbourhood for some time. He mentions flooding of the River Mole in October 1676 in his 'Tour through the whole Island of Great Britain'. Other eminent people are Francis Burney, Thomas Hope, the author of 'Anastasius' and collector of the famous Deepdene marbles, and diarist John Evelyn.

George Meredith lived at the foot of Box Hill from 1870 to 1909 and is buried in Dorking cemetery. Composer Dr. Ralph Vaughan Williams is another resident to which the town is indebted. Dorking is also associated with many quaint rituals and characters.

Shrove Tuesday football has long ceased. Everyone used to take part. The teams were formed of those living east and west of the church. The west end was the strongest and nearly always won. Each Shrove Tuesday, there were stirring scenes in the streets of the town, but the fun really began in earnest when the police authorities seriously attempted to put an end to the custom.

There have been some curious burials, too. For instance how many of the countless thousands who make Leith Hill the venue for an outing, and take the opportunity of ascending the tower, know that beneath their feet lie the bones of a wealthy politician and lawyer? He was Richard Hull, a gentleman of considerable estate in Ireland, who, in his time, was the oldest bencher of the Inner Temple and served for many years in the Parliament of Ireland. When he retired he went to live at Leith Hill Place, and having obtained the necessary permission from Sir John Evelyn, he built the tower on the summit of the hill. A few years later he died and in accordance with his wish, the tower from which he loved to drink in the beauty of nature, became his tomb for he was buried beneath a slab in its base.

The neighbouring height of Box Hill, however, can claim to have witnessed a more unusual interment. For it is here on the north-western brow, that a major of the Marines, lies head downwards. He was Peter Labelliere, who for some years lived at Dorking. In his younger days he was disappointed in love – so it is recorded – and as the years went by, his already unsettled mind was made the more unsettled by his dotings upon religion and politics. Finally his eccentricity obtained complete mastery, and he expressed the wish that he should be buried upside down, in order, he said, that 'as the world was turned topsy turvey, it was fit that he should be buried so, that he might be right at last'. The major's wish was observed and on the appointed day, 11 June 1800, crowds of people turned to watch this strange burial.

It is not known whether Labelliere would have objected to the occasion being made so public as it was; nor is it recorded that his perturbed spirit was the cause of certain mischievous promptings experienced by the youth of locality. But when the time came for the sightseers to return, they received a considerable shock. The little wooden bridge spanning the Mole had been broken down by boys and for many the only alternative to walking many miles was to wade through the none too inviting waters of the River Mole.

Dorking is also noted for its wealth of hostelries – best known is the White Horse, which existed long before 1552, when it was known as The Cross House.

On 1 May 1952, an 'Act for Keepers of Alehouses to be bound by Recognisance' came into effect. This Act forbade anyone to keep an alehouse except under licence from two justices of the peace. The justices were to take 'bond and surety' of twelve pence for each alehouse keeper 'for the maintenance of good order and rule'. A JP who took the twelve pence and failed to certify it at the next quarter sessions was to be fined £3-6s-8d.

An alehouse keeper who failed to conduct his house properly could be deprived of his bond at the quarter sessions and have his alehouse closed. Anyone keeping an alehouse without licence was to be imprisoned for three days. He could also be fined 20 shillings. Although the Act was repealed in 1829; it was the foundation of the licensing law as it is today.

In the fifties, Dorking boasted thirty hostelries among them the Red Lion Hotel situated in the centre of the High Street. Although featured in the list of antiquities prepared by the Records and Ancient monuments committee of the county council, the Red Lion closed in 1958 and the site was sold for redevelopment. The hotel was so called after the Arms of Arundels, who were Lords of the Manor at the time. It was not an ancient inn, but was on the site of one called The Cardinals Hat (or cap), the first mention of which is in a document dated 1427. The Cardinal in question was Henry Beaufort, son of John of Gaunt, who was Bishop of Winchester from 1404 to 1447, the year of his death. He was made a Cardinal in 1426.

Beneath Dorking's busy shopping streets, are a series of curious sand caves which, thanks to Dorking Preservation Society, have today become a real attraction. The original entrance to the caves, prior to 1919, was possibly tucked away behind cottages which at one time lined South Street. Cut out of solid sandrock, the caves are 50ft below the street surface. There is a staircase of fifty steps which have now been partially concreted since the Preservation Society took over the lease from the Council. Only half the width of the steps have been covered in order that visitors can still see the orginal surface. The caves are thought to have originally been used for the storage of smuggled goods brought from the coast. The oldest date found inscribed in the caves is 1672.

The author is grateful to her daughter Kay for typing all the text, also to Dorking Advertiser readers who over the years, have submitted many of the pictures and information; to Dorking Preservation Society and Dorking Museum.

1. Horses, pedal power and shank's pony dominated Dorking High Street when this picture was taken around the turn of the century. It was in the days when ladies' skirts swept the ground and there was a pub or grog shop every few yards.

2. The days when Dorking High Street was a pedestrian precinct – Market Day with animal pens on the cobblestones before the market was re-sited.

3. Cattle, sheep and poultry used to be the business of Dorking Market, pictured here in March 1926. Overflow animals were tied to the hitching rails which are still a feature of the High Street. But gradually the 'cheap jacks' moved in. And now the market offers a wide range of goods. The picture was taken from the Market Gate looking down towards Meadowbank.

4. This picture of Dorking High Street looking from Pump Corner is thought to have been taken either during or soon after the First World War – see the soldier with walking stick. The policeman at Pump Corner was a fixture for many years, dealing with traffic which met at the junction in the days when both West Street and South Street were two-way.

5. The Black Horse was a pub across the road from the White Horse in this early picture of the High Street. The Black Horse disappeared long ago, but the White Horse is still flourishing.

6. Shrove Tuesday football in the High Street about 1895. In the annual match, men from the eastern end of the town pitted themselves against men from the western end, struggling to get the ball to their own end of the town. As the church clock struck six, everyone stopped and the position of the ball decided the winners. The game grew in popularity over the years with hundreds taking part and spectators numbering more than 2,000. Violence escalated and shopkeepers boarded up their premises. The authorities finally decided to stop the game in 1898.

7. Massed ranks of uniformed policemen were there to keep the peace at the last official Shrove Tuesday football match in Dorking. Disappointed players are pictured heading back up South Street.

8. The last dancing bear in Dorking? This picture dated around 1900 was taken outside where Woolworths now stands.

9. Passionately fond of animals, Mrs. Elizabeth Spratley, pictured in a doorway of her husband's shop (now Clear's Electrical) with one of her cats. One of the town's great characters, she did not believe in paying water rates. She would supply all her needs from the town pump at Pump Corner.

10. Household goods and bric-à-brac shop used to be incorporated in the Spotted Dog pub building in South Street. Note the gate which is still there. The shop area is now the pub's lounge bar.

11. The town hung out the flags for the Silver Jubilee of their Majesties King George V and Queen Mary in 1935. Two years later the flags came out again for the Coronation of George VI.

12. Formerly the Market House, The Three Tuns Hotel pictured around eighty years ago, was replaced by a supermarket that now lies empty. The Three Tuns in the centre of the town used to be a favourite with farmers, who brought cattle to the neighbouring market. Before this, the cattle market took place twice weekly on the High Street cobbles and in the right foreground can be seen a cattle trough.

13. A political meeting on the steps of the Red Lion Hotel in 1913. In those days the hotel had its own garage and acted as an agent for Daimler hire.

14. The Red Lion just before it was demolished. Once during a particularly rowdy Shrove Tuesday football game in the street, the Riot Act was read from the doorway. But the building was swept away to be replaced by a shopping parade at the time when many of the town's pubs were closed.

15. Dene Street, formerly known as Ram Alley, after a pub which stood on the High Street corner, was at the turn of the century a cosy little jumble of small shops, pubs and cottages when this picture was taken. Traces of its old style remain today intermingled with new shops, and a small office block.

16. At one time, all the streets leading to the centre of Dorking town looked like West Street. But it alone has retained its appearance. A century ago, there was a toll bar across the bottom of West Street, which then had an even greater variety of inns. On the left can be seen the Kings Arms, which survives today along with the Old House at Home.

17. The Electric Theatre dominated the high side of South Street in the great days of silent films. When the talkies came, it was rebuilt as The Regent. But newer, plusher cinemas overtook it and it became auction rooms.

18. This early photograph of South Street shows the first home of Dorking General Post Office, later taken over by the JEA and Labour Exchange. The building was demolished in the early 1970s and rebuilt. The bandstand disappeared in the early 1960s.

19. South Street looking towards Pump Corner. On the right, the Bulls Head providing hospitality a century ago. Cyclists, tourists and commercial visitors were offered good food and accommodation. The premises of Messrs Crow, Watkin and Watkin, estate agents, who celebrated their centenary in 1986, is on the right.

20. The heavy Victorian buildings on the corner of Junction Road with South Street, once housed part of Dorking Urban Council and the Post Office. Further down South Street, is Beehive Cottage which used to stand next to the Spotted Dog. It had an attractive and unusually shaped roof. The small shops and cottages opposite were swept away when the street was widened and have been replaced by gardens and paved area.

21. This picture in the early thirties recalls the time when the No. 70 double-decker buses went up and down a two-way South Street and when Sondes Place Farm sold its dairy products from the shop opposite the bandstand. Near the bus is a shop festooned with boots – the dearest 6s 11d! Today the traffic is one way, heading west. Some of the shops pictured are still here, notably Rowes and Fullers.

22. The Methodist Church at South Street, large and impressive as it was, lasted a scant 72 years. It was built in 1901, but by the seventies the congregation were questioning the value of such a big building which would become increasingly more expensive to maintain. In 1973, the Methodists moved out to share St. Martin's Parish Church with the Anglican. With the money obtained for the Methodist Church site, St. Martin's church hall was added to and refurbished to become the interdenominational Christian Centre.

23. The horse trough in the middle of the five-road junction opposite the Falkland Arms, was put there to celebrate Queen Victoria's Golden Jubilee. Buses used to turn there and wait near the public house.

24. The Willow Walk by the Millpond in the Meadowbank recreation ground, used to be a romantic meeting place for the town's young men and women.

25. The area around the junction of London Road with High Street, has probably seen more change over the past eigthy years or so than any other part of the district. The little cottage advertising itself was a timber and builders' merchants, reached across almost as far as today's Service Station. The cottage went first, then the house behind that. Finally in the thirties, the junction was opened right out and the little country lane to Reigate became a four-lane highway.

26. A view down cottagy Mill Lane, at around 1905. No-one then could possibly have imagined the vast changes proposed for the surroundings, including the mini shopping complex in the market area behind on the left. The slopes of Ranmore can be seen in the background.

27. Cricket used to be played on Cotmandene – and a less likely site for the game would be hard to find with the ground sloping steeply away from a plateau. The home side who were used to it, took full advantage of their familiarity with the lie of the land. The game is believed to have started there in about 1780-1785, but towards the end of the 1870s moves were afoot to shift to the present ground at Pixham Lane. Cotmandene, given to the town by the Duke of Norfolk, was lavishly praised for the purity of its air by the author Daniel Defoe, who went to school in the town.

28. The tiny railway arch at Deepdene, disappeared when the bridge was widened to accommodate the dual carriageway in the sixties but at the time this picture was taken the road up to the Reigate Road roundabout, did not exist. Traffic went round via London Road. The picture was taken in the fifties when the old steam locomotives used to thunder along the Redhill-Reading line.

29. When the station known as Deepdene was first built at Dorking, it went by the misleading title of Box Hill. The reason was that the directors of the line wanted to attract some of the thousands of day trippers pouring out of the famous beauty spot at weekends and Bank Holidays. Never mind that the families faced quite a walk or the expense of a bus ride when they arrived!

30. The Star and Garter Hotel near Dorking North Station looked an entirely different place in the early years of this century when it featured an ornate verandah and a profusion of plants and flowers in pots and window boxes. Beyond it can be seen the old station, now replaced and incorporated into the Biwater office block.

31. The old Station Café at Dorking-North was a mecca for hikers, cyclists and taxi drivers. It disappeared when the station area was redeveloped with the Biwater office block, car park and new station entrance. For many years, it was owned by Mr. Arthur Searle.

32. The dual carriageway at Deepdene Avenue used to be a privately owned leafy lane, protected at either end by gates which was a short cut to Deepdene House. Lesser mortals had to go round via the London Road to join the Reigate Road. The tree-lined avenue broke off at the Reigate Road roundabout area and then resumed on the other side up to the house. The original road used to be on the left. The northbound carriageway was added later when the railway bridge over the road was widened.

33. Peaceful Rose Hill, just a few yards away from South Street, has changed little since the 19th century. Handsome houses, although many now converted into flats, still border the hill that offers commanding views of the north Downs. Entry to Rose Hill from South Street is through an archway which survives the march of time. It was originally the rear approach to the old mansion.

34. Pippbrook Mansion standing in 5½ acres of beautiful ground was bought as a new home for Dorking and District Council in 1930. This saved it from the house-breaker. Still a fine example of Gothic Renaissance style, it was officially opened as the council headquarters by the then Lord Lieutenant of Surrey, Lord Ashcombe, in 1931. Today it houses the town's library.

35. At the turn of the century, wooden cottages lined the roadside at Church Street. But they fell into disrepair to be replaced first by factory workshops and recently by Chapel Court complex of homes for the elderly.

36. St. Martin's Church as it appeared about 1890. The 200 ft spire to be seen today was built in memory of Bishop Wilberforce who was killed at Abinger in 1872 in a fall from his horse.

37. In the mid-1800s St. Martin's Church looked very different. This is the intermediate church; the ancient church dating from the Crusades was taken down in 1835-1837 and renewed, all but the chancel. Then in 1866 Henry Woodyer rebuilt the chancel, and in 1875, he rebuilt the work of 1835-1837.

38. St. Martin's vicarage on the corner of Vincent Lane and Westcott Road, is a fine Elizabethan building. Now turned into several individual residences, the vicarage remains today although the road has dropped considerably over the years as various alterations have been made.

39. Just behind the junctions of Vincent Lane, Coldharbour Lane and Falkland Road, stands St. Joseph's Roman Catholic Church much the same today as seventy years ago. Both the church and the attractive Georgian house on the corner have been preserved with loving care and the roads, although now covered with tarmac, follow the same course.

40. The Punchbowl Inn, Reigate Road, of the 1920s. In the background can be seen a meadow and woods where Overdale was built in the 1930s. And truly rural at the turn of the century, Punchbowl Lane when fields and hedgerows spanned the area. Later an estate of houses brought increased traffic.

41. In the early thirties, the site of the Indoor Market, South Street, was the Victory Tea Gardens. There, under the shade of a spreading tree, people sipped tea and ate dainty sandwiches and cakes, served by waitresses in a snow-white frilly cap and apron.

42. Going into hospital at Dorking used to be a cosy affair. Dorking Cottage Hospital in South Terrace had two main wards plus six beds for children and the town's general practitioners used to attend their own patients there and do their own operations. Fund raising for the hospital kept many people busy: Mr. Kibblewhite was one of the leading benefactors. Fresh air treatment was popular in the twenties. Beds were wheeled out on the verandah at the back of the buildings in all weathers.

43. Castle Mill, Dorking, on the banks of the river Mole, just below the A25 Reigate Road, suffered a serious fire in 1933. At the time, it was a working mill still grinding corn and run by 'Pug' Aldridge. Castle Mill is mentioned in the Domesday Book.

44. The old weir river from Castle Mill, Reigate Road, was a massive structure which allowed a deep, fast-flowing body of water to turn the heavy mill wheel. It has now been reconstructed further back beyond the bridge and provides a shallower flow, enough to turn the wheel, which has been adapted by the owners as a decorative feature today.

45. In the 1930s, the Watermill café-restaurant, as it was then, below Box Hill on the A25 Reigate Road was a popular roadhouse. Motorists would head for its hospitable terraces for tea and a dip in the pool and dance the night away to live bands. The pool has now been filled in and the building is a new one on the same site; the old one was destroyed by fire.

46. Deepdene House in the 1920s. At that time, Deepdene still retained some resemblance to the house which was one of England's stately homes for more than 100 years, visited by Royalty and Cabinet Ministers. The glory that once was Deepdene House was lost finally in 1968 when Federated Homes Ltd. bought the mansion from British Rail who moved their headquarters there during the war, for £100,000.

47. The area's most famous beauty spot is Box Hill. The first 230 acres including the summit of the hill, was presented to the nation by Leopold Solomons, JP, of Norbury Park, in 1914. Further land was given by others and bought by the National Trust. Jane Austen's 'Emma' describes a picnic on the slopes of the hill.

48. At the foot of Box Hill is the Burford Bridge Hotel, a fine old coaching inn that has had many distinguished visitors. Many believe that Lord Nelson stayed at the inn just before leaving for Trafalgar. Keats wrote 'Endymion' here.

49. Denbies mansion on the heights of Ranmore has been a feature of the Mole Valley landscape since the original house was built more than 200 years ago. Originally, Ranmore was known as Aschombe Hill and was farmed by a John Denby. In the 19th century on the slopes of Denbies, now devoted to vines, the limeworks still were in operation and provided some of the best lime in England for building purposes. As proof of the excellence, this lime was used in the erection of Somerset House, the Bank of England, London Bridge and the Houses of Parliament.

50. Estate workers from Bury Hill used to keep The Nower, in a cleared condition as a landscape park with mown grass and plenty of space between mature trees. It was presented to the town by Col. Robert Barclay in 1931 on the understanding that it should be left in its natural state, without flower beds, railings, gravel paths etc.

51. Burford Bridge has spread along the foot of Box Hill and added the Tithe Barn functions room since the twenties, when this picture was taken. It used to be the focal point for the Hunt's Boxing Day Meet when hundreds came on foot to see the horses and hounds. In the twenties it was a favourite stopping place for motoring runs.

52. Coldharbour Lane, Dorking, taken in about 1925. Then a narrow, unmade track, little more used than Falkland Grove serving the grand houses above it.

53. This picture taken in the churchyard at Wotton in the 1890s shows the ceremony of 'touching the Glanville stone' which had been in existence since about 1710. William Glanville, a nephew of diarist John Evelyn, left money in his will to be given each year to poor boys of the parish. At a date near his death in February, they gathered at this tomb to recite the Lords Prayer, Ten Commandments and Creed and were given about 40 shillings. Boys about to be apprenticed to a craft or trade were asked to write an essay on a quotation from the Bible and then qualified for £10 to equip themselves with tools. The custom lapsed some fifteen years ago partly through lack of suitable boys and partly through lack of interest. It had been brought back in 1977 and 1978 at the celebration of the church's millenium.

54. The turn of the century picture shows some sort of celebration or demonstration at Leith Hill Tower, the highest point in Surrey. Heads can be seen peering over the parapet and groups are standing on the grass below. The view from the top remains a constant source of delight and generations of children are still being told the tale that the tower brings the hill up to mountain height.

55. The Plough Inn, Coldharbour, is a welcome sight for travellers in the days when horse and carts were the main form of travel. Changes have been minimal over the years: a few more houses, a stable block village school converted to upmarket homes, but in the main the place is timeless.

56. Grazing animals on the common at Coldharbour kept the grass as tidy as a modern mower.

57. Friday Street used to be a busy little hamlet, with its own industries: farming, woodcutting etc.

58. The quaint old clock at Abinger Hammer remains a tourist attraction today. Projecting over the A25 road, on the hour, the smith strikes the time out with his hammer. A motto on the clock reads: 'By me you know how fast to go.'

59. Attractive rural Westcott Road presented an open vista about ninety years ago when this avenue of limes were little more than saplings and before the roads were made-up for heavy A25 traffic to spoil the scene. Box Hill rises in the background and what appears to be part of Broome Farm is on the right.

60. The Rookery, Westcott, a low rambling mansion, was famous as the Birthplace in 1766 of Thomas Malthus, who put forward the theory that mankind would outstrip the food supply of the planet unless something was done to curb the birthrate. In the sixties it was demolished to be replaced by Georgian-style homes.

61. A typical village school – South Holmwood (1905), when the handful of pupils played in the garden at the side of the building. Surrounded by fields, the tranquil environment is a far cry from the schools of today.

62. The village green and pond at North Holmwood around the turn of the century. Note the short grass nibbled down by livestock and the pond neatly edged and devoid of weeds and rushes.

63. Time has stood still for much of Brockham Village. Although Borough Bridge now serves more motorists as a crossing point over the River Mole, its single traffic lane remains. In November, thousands of visitors are attracted to Brockham Green's annual bonfire celebrations with torchlight processions through the village and firework display.

64. In the ninety years or so since this picture was taken, there has been little change in the appearance of this end of Mickleham. The houses still look out across Norbury Park from the terraced hillside and the pub still caters for locals who don't mind the rutted road. The biggest change is the main road itself which is now a dual carriageway and takes streams of heavy traffic.

65. Betchworth Castle is said to have been a place of some note in the 14th and 15th centuries, but in the reign of Queen Anne a considerable part of the building was pulled down and the rest converted into an ordinary mansion. This in turn became neglected, and when it came into the possession of the millionaire Hope family, it was finally dismantled.

66. Not such a far cry from today – Buckland Stores is still a favourite haunt of tourists as well as providing essential service for villagers. The store has been carefully maintained over the years and is noted for its delicious croissants! It is situated near the 14th century St. Mary's Church, that was restored during the last century.

67. Betchworth Church in the twenties. Much of the land around it was owned by Major General Coulbourn. The church contains several items of interest including an old chest cut out of a solid tree trunk and which is believed to be at least 1,000 years old.

68. The quaint old bus and the equally quaint old car were probably comparatively rare sights even in those days of uncluttered roads. Newdigate Village store itself appears not to have changed greatly since the thirties and it has been there since 1841. Before this it belonged to a butcher. The Old Bakery behind the shop has been removed brick by brick to the Singleton Open Air Museum, Sussex.

69. This picture was taken in 1905. Three young girls on an oasis where the unmade road divides in the centre of Newdigate Village. The village has a number of mature trees, some of which are reputed to be 500 years old. A local hostelry, the Surrey Oaks, dates back to the 15th century.

70. This old cottage in Partridge Lane, Newdigate, was demolished twenty years ago to the horror of historians. For it was said to be the oldest drovers' cottage in England, dating from 1430. Drovers moving herds of animals about the country used to sleep at the cottage and water their sheep or cattle at the nearby pond.

71. Yesteryear at Capel. Carters was then a haven for cyclists when the only other means of transport through the village were horse-drawn vehicles. The neighbouring timber houses have been carefully preserved along with several other 15th, 16th and 17th century structures.

72. Flint Cottage, Box Hill, was built at the beginning of the 19th century. Novelist and poet George Meredith came to live here soon after his second marriage in 1864 and died here on 18 May 1909. Meredith built the chalet, standing higher on the hill above the house, in 1876. After Meredith, Mr. and Mrs. Ralph Wood lived there until their deaths in 1945. Mr. M.E. Ruffer took possession in 1946 and on behalf of his sister, Mrs. Ralph Wood, gave the cottage to the National Trust.

73. Men of the London Scottish are pictured at a kit inspection at Rothes Road, where they were billeted in 1916 before taking the train bound for France. Many were killed and for years after the war the regiment held an annual memorial service in the town, combining it with manoeuvres at Ranmore. Older Dorkinians remember marching behind them as young boys and searching for cartridge cases on the common.

74. Bartholomew Press, South Street, off to Brighton for their annual trip to the coast in the mid-1920s. The Press employed some highly skilled workers who dealt with specialist medical printing for Bartholomew Hospital. The char-à-banc was owned and driven by Mr. Lipscombe of Junction Road, Dorking.

75. A fire chief's funeral passing through the centre of Dorking town in 1898. Walking just in front of the horse-drawn carriage is the top hatted Albert Whyatt, second son of Thomas Henry Sherlock.

76. Dorking has always boasted a high number of soccer fans. The local football club is the sixth oldest club in the country and the second oldest in Surrey, the original team kicked off in the Redhill and District League. Pictured, Dorking Football team 1907-1908 – winners of the Mid-Surrey League and runners-up for the Surrey Charity Cup.